the
TRICITY
cookery
book

PART NO. 84785/5/66

THORN

A member of the Thorn Group

TRICITY COOKERS LIMITED
NEW LANE, HAVANT, HAMPSHIRE
HAVANT 6400   STD 0701-2 6400

introduction

This book of recipes has been produced to help you in achieving the very best results from your Tricity Cooker. It will enable you to prepare meals and dishes to delight the people for whom you cook and of which you will be justly proud.

If you are new to electric cooking you will find it particularly advantageous to consult the cooking chart in the Operating Instructions for the cooking period, temperature setting, oven shelf position, etc., for each recipe, but in time these will become second nature to you. The Instructions also tell you how simply your cooker is operated and how to keep it clean and in tip-top condition. If you follow these simple instructions you can rely on your Tricity Cooker for years of trouble-free and excellent service.

Please remember that Tricity are genuinely interested in you, the purchaser. Our Staff, whether Housecraft Advisers, Sales or Service, will always be pleased to give advice that will help you to get the maximum satisfaction from your Cooker.

contents

weighing and measuring

It is most important to weigh and measure ingredients correctly if success is to be assured.

When buying scales, purchase a good pair and they will last a lifetime.

When the correct weight is measured, the scale pan should see-saw up and down, not come to rest permanently down.

Standard measuring spoons should be used. If these are not available, use an average sized teaspoon, dessertspoon and tablespoon.

Handy Measures

1 oz. flour	3 level tablespoons
1 oz. caster sugar	1½ level tablespoons
1 oz. grated cheese	2 level tablespoons
1 oz. cocoa	3 level tablespoons
1 oz. cornflour	3 level tablespoons
1 oz. jam	1 level tablespoon
1 oz. golden syrup	1 level tablespoon
1 oz. dried fruit	2 level tablespoons
1 oz. breadcrumbs	5 level tablespoons

Size of dishes

Sizes of ovenware dishes are measured by their liquid capacity.

e.g. 2 pints water poured into a 2 pint dish will come up to the rim.

Temperatures

For various reasons you may wish to know how the temperature settings on your electric cooker compare with other methods of expressing oven heat.

Thermostat Setting °F.				Regulo (approx.)
250°	..	..	..	..	$\frac{1}{2}$ ⎱ Very cool
275°	..	..	..	..	1 ⎰
300°	..	..	..	..	2—Cool
325°	..	..	..	..	3—Warm
350°	..	..	..	..	4—Moderate
375°	..	..	..	..	5 ⎱ Fairly hot
400°	..	..	..	..	6 ⎰
425°	..	..	..	..	7—Hot
450°	..	..	..	..	8 ⎱ Very hot
475°	..	..	..	..	9 ⎰

cooking terms

Blanching	Place food in boiling water for a few minutes then plunge into cold water. Blanching partly cooks food.
Blend	To mix thoroughly. When instructed to blend flour etc., with water, cold water should be added drop by drop, mixing well until a smooth thin paste is obtained.
Coat	To cover with a thin layer.
Frying	*Shallow Frying.* Use enough fat to cover base of pan. *Deep Frying.* Some fats give off a blue haze as they reach high temperature. However, this is not so with modern oils and should therefore not be used as a rough temperature guide. The use of a thermo-

meter is recommended. As a rough temperature guide—fry a cube of bread; it should rise to the surface and brown within one minute.

1. Use a deep fat pan which covers the whole of the radiant ring area.
2. Do not fill pan more than $\frac{1}{3}$ full of fat or oil.
3. It is advisable to remove the lid from the pan both while the fat is heating and during cooking.
4. Never leave the pan unattended while being used. If called away, switch off heat.
5. Always dry food before deep fat frying.
6. To prevent bubbling over, add food in small quantities and lower gradually into hot fat.

Garnish To trim or decorate.

Grate To shave into thin shreds using a grater.

Grilling Brush over prepared food with olive oil or melted fat. Preheat the grill at 'FULL' until red hot. Grease the grid and place food in position. Grill quickly on each side for 2 minutes, reduce the heat and continue to cook for the required length of time, turning occasionally.
The grill can be used to brown top of cheese dishes etc. Eggs may also be grilled. Lightly grease grill pan, pre-heat grill with pan in position, carefully place eggs in the pan and cook for the required time basting when necessary.

Raspings (a) Finely grate stale bread crumbs.
(b) Lightly brown thin slices of bread in oven. Crush.
(c) Use commercially prepared 'Golden Crumbs'.

Seasoned Flour Sieve together 1 tablespoonful flour, 1 teaspoonful salt and $\frac{1}{4}$ teaspoonful pepper.

Simmer Liquid simmers when an occasional bubble only appears on the surface.

Steaming (a) Place food in a 'steamer' (a special pan with holes in base) over a pan of boiling water.
(b) Place a deep enamel plate over a pan of boiling water. Arrange food on the plate, add a little liquid and cover with a lid.

Stock A well flavoured liquid made by:
(a) Boiling bones, meat, vegetables or fish together slowly. Strain.
(b) Dissolving commercially prepared 'stock cubes' in water.

recipes

batters

yorkshire pudding

1. Sieve flour and salt into a mixing bowl.
2. Make a 'well' in the flour, drop in the beaten egg. Stir, with a circular motion, taking a little flour down from the edge each time. Add a little milk, continue to stir and add more milk until all the flour is mixed in and a smooth batter is obtained.
3. Beat for 5 minutes. Stir in remaining milk, cover and leave to stand for 1 hour before cooking.
4. Melt lard in tin, when hot, pour in batter. Bake.

INGREDIENTS
4 oz. plain flour
1 egg
½ pint milk
Pinch salt
1 oz. lard

coating batter

This batter is suitable for coating Fruit Fritters or fish to be deep fried.

Make up mixture as for Yorkshire Pudding using ¼ pint liquid only.

pancakes

1. Make up as for Yorkshire Pudding.
2. Place a little lard in a frying pan and heat.
3. Pour spoonfuls of the batter into the pan. Spread by tilting. Fry gently until underside is lightly browned, toss or turn. Cook lightly on the second side.
4. Sprinkle with caster sugar and serve at once with lemon wedges.

These may be served with syrup or jam.

INGREDIENTS
Yorkshire pudding
  mixture
Lard
Lemon
Caster sugar

individual yorkshire puddings

Make up mixture as for Yorkshire Pudding.
Place small knobs of lard in patty tins. Heat.
Pour a little mixture into each. Bake. Sufficient
for approx. 18 puddings.

sausage toad

Make up mixture as for Yorkshire Pudding.
Pour batter into hot fat, carefully arrange
sausages in the mixture (first remove skins).
Bake.

INGREDIENTS
12 oz. sausages

 # biscuits

biscuits

1. Cream fat and sugar together.
2. Sieve flour and salt.
3. Fold flour into creamed mixture.
4. Stir until mixture forms a dough, knead up.
   Roll out ¼″ thick and using a 2″ cutter, shape
   into biscuits (18–20). Place on baking tray,
   prick well. Bake.

INGREDIENTS
6 oz. plain flour
4½ oz. margarine or
  butter
1½ oz. icing sugar
Pinch salt

currant biscuits

Make up mixture as for Biscuits, sieving spice
with flour and salt. Add currants to creamed
mixture before adding flour.

INGREDIENTS
3 oz. currants
½ level teaspoonful
  mixed spice

lemon biscuits

Make up mixture as for Biscuits (see previous page) adding rind to creamed mixture before adding flour.

INGREDIENTS
**Rind of 1 lemon
(finely grated)**

orange biscuits

Make up mixture as for Biscuits (see previous page) adding rind to creamed mixture before adding flour.

INGREDIENTS
**Rind of 1 orange
(finely grated)
Rind of ½ lemon
(finely grated)**

All the above mixtures may be shaped with fancy cutters and coated with flavoured Glacé Icing (page 38).

shortbread

Make up Biscuit mixture (see previous page) substituting ground rice for 1 oz. flour. After kneading up, roll out to a circle 7″ in diameter. Press into the tin. Prick well. Bake.

INGREDIENTS
1 oz. ground rice

cheese biscuits

1. Sieve flour, salt, mustard and pepper together.
2. Rub fat into flour. Add cheese.
3. Add sufficient beaten egg to form a pliable dough.
4. Roll out pastry ⅛″ thick and using a 2″ cutter, shape biscuits.
5. Arrange on a baking tray, prick well. Bake.

INGREDIENTS
**6 oz. plain flour
4 oz. margarine
4 oz. strong cheese
(finely grated)
Beaten egg to bind
Pinch salt, pepper and
dry mustard**

cheese straws

Make up mixture as above. Roll out cheese pastry ⅛″ thick and cut into thin strips about 3″ long. Arrange pastry strips on baking tray, lined with greaseproof paper. Bake.

Cakes may be divided into the following classes, depending on the proportion of various ingredients.

The method of mixing and blending is influenced by these proportions.

Plain Cakes   in which the fat is rubbed into the flour. This type is economical to make, but becomes stale after a day or so, due to the low fat content.

Rich Cakes   in which the fat and sugar are beaten together, more fat and eggs give good keeping qualities.

Sponge Cakes   in which the eggs and sugar are whisked together to a thick cream. Best eaten when fresh due to low fat content.

Gingerbread   in which the fat is melted. This mixture improves in flavour during storage.

preparation of tins

Bun or patty tins   Lightly grease, using melted fat.

Sandwich tins   Cut a disc of greaseproof paper to fit the base, grease paper and side of tins with melted fat.

Sandwich tins for sponge mixtures   Grease tin well with melted fat. Sprinkle with a mixture of equal quantity flour and caster sugar. This method is also used for a sponge flan tin.

Swiss roll tin   Cut a piece of greaseproof paper 1″ larger over-all than the tin. Make a short cut, 1″ in from each end along the short sides. Place the paper in the tin, grease very well, using melted fat. Tuck the cut corners in neatly.

Deep round   Cut a greaseproof paper circle to fit the base of the tin, also a strip for the sides, 1″ deeper than the cake tin. Taking the long strip, make a ½″ fold along the edge, make cuts at intervals, cutting up to the fold line. Place this strip round the side of the tin, (the folded, cut portion fits in the base and forms 'pleats') lay the circle in the base. Grease well with melted fat.

Deep square   Cut two pieces of greaseproof paper, the width of the tin, and the length to equal base plus sides. Place one piece in one direction and the other in the opposite direction. Grease well with melted fat.

mixing the cake

Beating   *thick mixtures* Use a wooden spoon, tilt the bowl slightly, rest on a folded tea-towel to keep bowl in a firm position.

thin mixtures Use a hand or rotary whisk.

Creaming   Use a wooden spoon, break up fat, add the sugar and beat well.
In cold weather when the fat is hard, warm the sugar slightly to make creaming easier.

Folding in   Use a metal spoon to cut through and through the mixture giving an occasional stir. This is a method of mixing the ingredients in the lightest possible way.
Continue until a smooth mixture is obtained.

| **Rubbing in** | Cut the fat into small pieces, add to the flour. Using the finger tips, pick up the flour and fat, rub together lightly. When mixture resembles fine breadcrumbs, proceed as directed in recipe. |

| **Sieving** | This ensures thorough mixing of all dry ingredients, removal of any lumps present in flour and introduces air into the mixture, thus making it light. |

ingredients

| **Dried fruit** | Wash well, pick over. Cover a cake rack with absorbent kitchen paper or muslin. Spread fruit on prepared rack, stand in warm place to dry. Chop large raisins, ginger, dates, nuts, glacé cherries etc. |

| **Eggs** | Break one at a time into a cup to test for freshness. Beat well before adding to mixture unless otherwise instructed.
Weigh or measure all ingredients very carefully. |

consistency

| **Stiff** | Mixture too sticky to handle, keeps shape when dropped from a spoon.
Plainer cakes and puddings are usually mixed to this consistency. |

| **Soft** | Mixture should readily drop from spoon when shaken, but is much too thick to pour. |

| **Pouring** | A batter-like consistency, obtained when making Swiss Rolls and Gingerbreads. |

cooking and cooling

| **Testing** | Press lightly with finger tips, if cooked the mixture feels 'springy', looks risen and brown. Larger cakes shrink slightly from the edge. Large cakes may also be tested by placing a warm skewer in the centre which will be quite clean when withdrawn if cooking is complete. |

Cooling small cakes	Remove from oven, leave for a few minutes. Remove from tin and place on a cooling rack.
Cooling large cakes	Remove from oven, leave in tin until cool. Remove from tin carefully and place on cooling rack. Remove paper. Make sure cake is quite cold before storing in a cake tin.

bakewell tart

1. Make up pastry (page 54). Roll out and line sandwich tin. Spread base with jam.
2. Cream margarine and sugar until light and 'fluffy'.
3. Gradually add lightly beaten egg. Add a little at a time, beat in well between each addition.
4. Beat in essences.
5. Fold in ground almonds and cake crumbs, stir well. Cover jam with this mixture.
6. Roll out pastry scraps and cut into thin strips. Place on top, lattice fashion. Bake.

INGREDIENTS
6 oz. flan pastry
1 egg
2 oz. margarine
2 oz. caster sugar
1 oz. ground almonds
1½ oz. cake crumbs
¼ teaspoonful vanilla essence
½ teaspoonful almond essence
Jam

christmas cake

1. Line tin.
2. Prepare the fruit, wash and dry if necessary, chop glacé cherries, blanch, skin and chop almonds.
3. Cream margarine with sugar until light and 'fluffy'.
4. Gradually add lightly beaten eggs. Add a little at a time, beating well between each addition.
5. Beat in essences, liquid and rind.
6. Add almonds and cherries. Beat.
7. Sieve flour, salt and spice together.
8. Add half quantity flour and fruit to creamed mixture and fold in.
9. Add remainder of flour and fruit. Continue to stir until all ingredients are blended together.
10. Place mixture in prepared tin, smooth top of cake. Bake.

NOTE
When cooking very large Christmas cakes reduce the temperature by 25° after the first 4 hours cooking time. Alternatively cook at 25° lower for the entire cooking period.

INGREDIENTS
12 oz. currants
2 oz. whole almonds
4 oz. glacé cherries
10 oz. sultanas
4 oz. mixed chopped peel
6 oz. caster sugar
6 oz. raisins
10 oz. plain flour
8 oz. margarine or butter
1-2 teaspoonfuls mixed spice
½ lemon rind (finely grated)
½ orange rind (finely grated)
¼ teaspoonful salt
1-3 tablespoonfuls liquid (may be spirit, fruit juice or milk)
4 eggs
Vanilla, rum, almond and coffee essence. A few drops of each

congress tarts

1. Make up pastry (page 54) and set aside.
2. Mix margarine and sugar using a fork.
3. Lightly beat egg and almond essence together, add to margarine and sugar mixture, beating well. Continue to beat until a smooth consistency is obtained.
4. Fold in ground rice.
5. Roll out pastry and line patty tins, using a 3″ cutter.
6. Place a little jam in the base of each, place a heaped teaspoonful of the filling on top of the jam. Smooth over.
7. Roll out pastry scraps and cut a few thin strips. Place these on top of tarts crosswise. Bake. Sufficient for 10 tarts.

INGREDIENTS
4 oz. shortcrust pastry
Filling
3 oz. caster sugar
1 oz. margarine
3 oz. ground rice
1 small egg
¼ teaspoonful almond essence
Raspberry jam

fruit cake

1. Line tin.
2. Cream margarine and sugar until light and 'fluffy'.
3. Gradually add lightly beaten eggs. Add a little at a time, beating well between each addition.
4. Sieve flour, salt and baking powder together.
5. Sieve flour into creamed mixture, add fruit and fold in.
6. Add water and continue to stir until all ingredients are blended together.
7. Place mixture in prepared tin, smooth top. Bake.

INGREDIENTS
9 oz. plain flour
5 oz. margarine
5 oz. caster sugar
6 oz. mixed dried fruit
2 eggs
1½ level teaspoonfuls baking powder
Pinch salt
1-2 tablespoonfuls water

madeira cake

Make up mixture as for previous recipe, omitting fruit and adding lemon rind to creamed mixture. Place the citron peel on the top of the cake after first 20 minutes cooking time.

INGREDIENTS
Rind of 1 lemon (finely grated)
Citron peel

cherry cake

Make up mixture as for Fruit Cake, omitting dried fruit and adding chopped cherries and essences to creamed mixture.

INGREDIENTS
4 oz. glacé cherries
Vanilla essence
Almond essence

walnut cake

Make up mixture as for Fruit Cake, omitting dried fruit and adding walnuts and essence to creamed mixture.

INGREDIENTS
4 oz. chopped walnuts
Vanilla essence

macaroons

1. Whisk egg white, ground almonds, caster sugar and essences together for 10 minutes.
2. Fold in ground rice.
3. Place in teaspoonfuls on a baking tray lined with rice paper. Top with split almond if desired. Bake. (Approx. 10 biscuits.)

INGREDIENTS
1 oz. ground almonds
4 oz. caster sugar
1 egg white
1 oz. ground rice
½ teaspoonful vanilla essence
½ teaspoonful almond essence
Whole almonds (optional)

gingerbread

1. Grease tin.
2. Sieve flour, salt and spices.
3. Place milk, sugar, syrup, treacle, and margarine in a saucepan. Leave over a gentle heat to melt but do not allow to become very hot.
4. Pour melted mixture on to flour, beat well. Add lightly beaten eggs. Beat until mixture is smooth. The consistency should be that of a thick batter. Add a little more milk if required.
5. Pour into prepared tin. Bake.

INGREDIENTS
12 oz. self raising flour
6 oz. margarine
4 oz. caster sugar
2 eggs
4 tablespoonfuls milk
3 tablespoonfuls golden syrup
1 tablespoonful black treacle
1½ level teaspoonfuls ground ginger
Pinch cinnamon
Pinch salt
Pinch mixed spice

mixed fruit gingerbread

Make up mixture as for previous recipe, adding fruit to flour before adding melted mixture.

INGREDIENTS
8 oz. mixed dried fruit

gingerbread special

Make up mixture as for Gingerbread, adding coarsely chopped crystallised ginger to flour before adding melted mixture.

When cake is cooked and quite cold, slice through and spread with filling and sandwich together. Spread Glacé Icing (page 38) over the top and decorate with thin slices of crystallised ginger.

INGREDIENTS
4-6 oz. crystallised ginger
Glacé icing

Filling
Thick honey blended with sufficient ground almonds to form a spreadable mixture

meringues

1. Whisk egg whites until stiff.
2. Add half sugar and continue beating.
3. Fold in remaining sugar.
4. Place in spoonfuls or pipe onto baking tray lined with lightly oiled greaseproof paper. Bake until dried out.
5. When cold, sandwich together with double cream.

INGREDIENTS
4 oz. caster sugar
2 egg whites
Double cream (whipped)

mixed fruit cakes

1. Sieve flour, spice and salt.
2. Rub in margarine. Stir in sugar, fruit and peel.
3. Add lightly beaten eggs, also 1 tablespoonful milk. Mix to a stiff consistency, adding more milk if necessary.
4. Place mixture into lightly greased patty tins. Bake.

INGREDIENTS
10 oz. self raising flour
5 oz. margarine
5 oz. caster sugar
2 eggs
Pinch salt
4 oz. sultanas
2 oz. currants
1 oz. mixed peel
$\frac{1}{2}$ level teaspoonful mixed spice

date and lemon cakes

Omit spice, peel and fruit from the previous recipe.

Make up mixture, adding lemon rind and dates with sugar. Substitute lemon juice for part milk.

INGREDIENTS

Rind of 1 lemon (finely grated)

3 oz. coarsely chopped dates

Juice of ½ lemon

ginger cakes

1. Cream margarine with sugar until light and 'fluffy'.
2. Gradually add lightly beaten eggs. Add a little at a time, beating well between each addition.
3. Sieve flour, salt, baking powder and ginger.
4. Sieve flour onto creamed mixture, add crystallised ginger. Stir gently until all ingredients are blended together.
5. Place mixture into lightly greased patty tins. Bake.

INGREDIENTS

8 oz. plain flour

5 oz. margarine

5 oz. caster sugar

2 eggs

Pinch salt

1½ level teaspoonfuls baking powder

1 level teaspoonful ground ginger

2-4 oz. coarsely chopped crystallised ginger

walnut and coffee cakes

Omit ginger from previous recipe.

Make up mixture, adding coffee essence to beaten egg. Add walnuts with flour.

INGREDIENTS

3 oz. coarsely chopped walnuts

1-2 teaspoonfuls coffee essence

victoria sandwich

1. Line tins.
2. Cream margarine with sugar, until light and 'fluffy'.
3. Gradually add lightly beaten eggs. Add a little at a time, beating well between each addition.
4. Sieve flour and salt.
5. Fold flour into creamed mixture, stir gently until a smooth consistency is obtained.
6. Divide mixture and place in prepared tins. Bake.
7. When cooked, cool, spread with jam and sandwich together.

INGREDIENTS
4 oz. self raising flour
4 oz. margarine
4 oz. caster sugar
2 eggs
Pinch salt
Raspberry jam

chocolate sandwich

Make up mixture as for previous recipe, sieving cocoa with flour and salt before folding into creamed mixture.

When cool, sandwich together with Chocolate Butter Icing (page 38).

INGREDIENTS
1 oz. cocoa
Chocolate butter icing

coffee sandwich

Make up mixture as for Victoria Sandwich. Adding instant coffee powder to margarine and sugar before creaming.

When cool, sandwich together with Coffee Butter Icing (page 38).

INGREDIENTS
1 level tablespoonful instant coffee powder
Coffee butter icing

orange sandwich

Make up mixture as for Victoria Sandwich. Add orange and lemon rind to creamed mixture. When cool, sandwich together with Orange Butter Icing (page 37).

INGREDIENTS
Rind of 1 orange (finely grated)
Rind of ½ lemon (finely grated)
Orange butter icing

lemon sandwich

Make up mixture as for Victoria Sandwich. Add lemon rind to creamed mixture. When cool, sandwich together with Lemon Butter Icing (page 37).

INGREDIENTS
Rind of 1 lemon (finely grated)
Lemon butter icing

sponge sandwich

1. Prepare tins.
2. Whisk eggs and sugar together for 10 minutes or until mixture is thick and creamy.
3. Sieve flour and salt together, sieve half quantity of flour onto whisked mixture. Fold in gently.
4. Add warm water and stir in. Sieve in remaining flour and fold in as before. Continue to stir until a smooth consistency is obtained.
5. Pour into prepared tins. Bake.
6. Remove from tins and cool. When quite cold, sandwich together with Butter Icing (page 37).

INGREDIENTS
3 oz. plain flour
3 oz. caster sugar
3 eggs
1 tablespoonful warm water
Pinch salt
Butter icing

chocolate sponge sandwich

Make up mixture as for previous recipe, sieving cocoa with flour and salt before folding into whisked mixture. When adding water, slightly more may be required to make correct consistency.

INGREDIENTS
1 oz. cocoa

swiss roll

1. Line tin.
2. Whisk eggs and sugar together for 10 minutes or until mixture is thick and creamy.
3. Sieve flour and salt together, sieve half quantity of flour onto whisked mixture. Fold in gently.
4. Add warm water and stir in. Sieve in remaining flour and fold in as before. Continue to stir until smooth consistency is obtained.
5. Pour into prepared tin. Bake.

INGREDIENTS
2 oz. plain flour
2 oz. caster sugar
2 eggs
1 tablespoonful warm water
Pinch salt
Jam

To Roll

Place a piece of greaseproof paper approx. 9″ × 12″ over a damp cloth. Just before removing Swiss Roll from oven, sprinkle paper with caster sugar.

Remove Swiss Roll from oven, turn onto sugared paper. Remove lining paper, spread Swiss Roll with warm jam. Roll carefully and leave to cool on a cake rack.

chocolate swiss roll

Make up mixture as for previous recipe, sieving cocoa with flour and salt before folding into whisked mixture.

Roll as above, but roll paper in with cake (do not add jam). When cake is cold, unroll carefully and spread with Butter Icing (page 37). Roll up carefully and sprinkle with icing sugar.

INGREDIENTS
3-5 level teaspoonfuls cocoa
Butter icing

cream and jam swiss roll

Make up mixture as for Swiss Roll. Finish as for Chocolate Swiss Roll but spread with jam and cream.

INGREDIENTS
Double cream (whipped)
Jam

fish

preparation

Flat Fish   Remove head and entrails. Wash fish well, using salt to clean away dark skin.

Round Fish   Remove head, make a slit on the underside towards the tail, remove entrails. Wash fish well, using salt to clean away dark skin.

Other preparation   Remove fins and loose scales. Replace roe if desired. Dry.

methods of cooking fish

baked fish

Place prepared fish on a baking tray or in an oven-ware dish. Sprinkle with seasoning and lemon juice. Dot with butter or margarine. Cover with greased paper.

Thin pieces of fish, e.g. fillets, may be placed on greaseproof paper for easy removal. Fold, roll or place in layers to keep moist during cooking.

Allow 10–30 minutes depending on thickness of fish. To test, insert a knife in a thick part, which should look creamy white when cooked. See your Instruction Card for temperature and oven position. Serve with sauce, e.g., parsley, anchovy, etc.

baked stuffed fish

Prepare fish, spread and roll or fill the cavity with Parsley and Thyme stuffing (page 89). Cover and see your Instruction Card for temperature and oven position.

steamed fish

Steaming is suitable for fillets and fish steaks. Prepare fish, season and sprinkle with lemon juice. Steam. To test, insert a knife in a thick part, which should look creamy white when cooked. Serve with sauce, e.g., parsley, anchovy, etc.

grilled fish

Grilling is suitable for herrings, mackerel, kippers, flat fish and fish steaks.

Prepare fish, cut to allow the heat to penetrate, grill. Oily fish such as herrings do not need to be brushed with oil, but white fish such as sole and plaice etc., require to be brushed liberally with melted fat or oil before and during grilling. To test, insert a knife in a thick part, which should look creamy white when cooked. Serve with sauce, e.g., parsley, anchovy, etc.

fried fish

Deep frying is suitable for fillets, small steaks and small whole fish. Shallow frying is suitable for thicker pieces of fish and all oily fish.

Prepare fish, season, and coat with seasoned flour, egg and breadcrumbs or Coating Batter (page 16).

poached fish

Poaching is suitable for fillets, fish steaks and small whole fish.

Prepare fish, place in saucepan containing a small amount of boiling water. To test, insert a knife in a thick part, which should look creamy white when cooked. Remove carefully, to facilitate this the fish may be tied in a piece of muslin before cooking. Serve with sauce, e.g., parsley, anchovy, etc.

baked stuffed cod

1. Wipe fish carefully and remove bone and fins.
2. Make up stuffing (page 89).
3. Stuff bone cavity. Tie steaks round with string.
4. Coat fish with flour, brush with beaten egg, cover with raspings. Place on a baking tray, cover with a piece of greased greaseproof paper. Bake.
   Remove string. Serve decorated with lemon slices and parsley.

INGREDIENTS
4 cod steaks
**Parsley and thyme
   stuffing**
Seasoning
Coating
**Flour, beaten egg,
   raspings**
Garnish
**Lemon slices and
   parsley**

baked stuffed plaice

1. Prepare fish. With the white side uppermost, make a 4″ cut along the backbone. Work the knife out towards the sides between the flesh and bone to form a 'pocket'.
2. Make up stuffing (page 89) use to fill 'pocket'.
3. Coat fish with flour, brush with beaten egg and cover with raspings. Place on a baking tray, cover with a piece of greased grease-proof paper. Bake.
   Serve with lemon slices and parsley.

INGREDIENTS
1 large plaice
Seasoning
**Parsley and thyme
   stuffing**
Coating
**Flour, beaten egg,
   raspings**
Garnish
**Lemon slices and
   parsley**

fish cakes

1. Mash fish, remove bones. Mash potatoes. Mix together with egg, lemon, seasoning and parsley.
2. Place on a floured board and divide into 6. Shape each portion into a flat round cake.
3. Coat with flour, egg and raspings. Fry in hot fat until heated through. Serve with Parsley Sauce.

INGREDIENTS
8 oz. cooked fish
4 oz. cooked potatoes
½ egg
**Juice and finely grated
   rind of ½ lemon**
Seasoning
**½ teaspoonful chopped
   parsley**
Coating
**Flour, beaten egg,
   raspings**

russian fish pie

1. Make up pastry (page 53). Make up White Sauce (page 69 half quantity).
2. Mix fish, first remove skin and bones, White Sauce, parsley, lemon juice and seasoning together.
3. Roll out pastry into a square 12″ × 12″. Trim edges. Place on a baking tray. Place the filling in the centre. Damp edges, fold each corner into the centre, forming an envelope. Seal edges, brush with beaten egg.
4. Cut leaves from remaining pastry, place along joins, brush leaves with beaten egg. Carefully lift leaf and make small incisions at each join, this will allow steam to escape and pastry will be more crisp and light. Bake.

INGREDIENTS
8 oz. flaky pastry
12 oz. cooked fish
¼ pint white sauce
1 dessertspoonful chopped parsley
2 teaspoonfuls lemon juice
Seasoning
Beaten egg

savoury cod

1. Fry onion lightly in margarine. (Use 7″–8″ saucepan.)
2. Add stock, cinnamon, rice and sultanas. Bring to the boil, cover with a lid and simmer gently for 10 minutes.
3. Wash fish, remove skin and cut into ½″ cubes. Lay fish on top of rice, sprinkle with salt. Continue to cook slowly until fish is cooked and stock is absorbed, about 30 minutes. Serve with lemon juice or Soy Sauce.

INGREDIENTS
1½ oz. margarine
1 large onion (finely chopped)
4 oz. Patna rice
¾ pint fish stock
Pinch cinnamon
¼ teaspoonful salt
4 oz. sultanas
1 lb. cod

soused herrings or mackerel

1. Prepare fish, place in dish.
2. Add salt, mace, bay leaf, peppercorns and cloves. Pour over vinegar and water. Cover with a piece of greased greaseproof paper. Bake.

INGREDIENTS
4 fresh herrings or mackerel
¼ teaspoonful salt
1 blade mace
1 bay leaf
8 peppercorns
3 cloves
Mixture of equal quantities water and vinegar, enough to cover fish

icings

almond icing

Sufficient to cover 8″ round cake.
1. Whisk eggs and essences together. Whisk in sugar.
2. Stir in ground almonds. Adjust consistency by adding a little extra egg or ground almonds until mixture resembles a pliable dough, but is not sticky. Knead well.

If not required to be used at once, wrap well in waxed paper and keep in a cool place.

INGREDIENTS
1 lb. ground almonds
8 oz. caster sugar
8 oz. icing sugar
Almond essence
Vanilla essence
Orange flower water
2-3 eggs (according to size)

butter icing

1. Sieve icing sugar.
2. Cream butter, add sieved icing sugar, a little at a time, beating well. Add essence, mix thoroughly.

INGREDIENTS
4 oz. butter
8 oz. icing sugar
Vanilla essence

orange butter icing

Make up mixture as above, substituting orange rind for essence.

INGREDIENTS
Rind of ½ orange (finely grated)

lemon butter icing

Make up mixture as above, substituting lemon rind for essence.

INGREDIENTS
Rind of ½ lemon (finely grated)

37

coffee butter icing

Cream butter and beat in coffee essence. Add sieved icing sugar a little at a time, beating well.

INGREDIENTS
2 teaspoonfuls coffee essence
4 oz. butter
8 oz. icing sugar

chocolate butter icing

Sieve drinking chocolate with icing sugar. Cream butter and beat in coffee essence. Add icing sugar/chocolate a little at a time, beating well. Add a little water to make a spreading consistency.

INGREDIENTS
1½-2 tablespoonfuls drinking chocolate
½ teaspoonful coffee essence
Water
4 oz. butter
8 oz. icing sugar

glacé icing

1. Sieve icing sugar, add sufficient water to make a stiff pouring consistency.
2. Beat well and add colouring as required.

INGREDIENTS
8 oz. icing sugar
Water
Colouring

orange glacé icing

Make up mixture as for previous recipe, using strained orange juice in place of water.

INGREDIENTS
Orange juice

lemon glacé icing

Make up mixture as for Glacé Icing, using strained lemon juice in place of water.

INGREDIENTS
Lemon juice

coffee glacé icing

Make up mixture as for Glacé Icing (page 38), using coffee essence and a little water in place of all water. The amount of coffee depends on strength of essence and individual taste.

(page 38)

INGREDIENTS
Coffee essence
Water

chocolate glacé icing

1. Blend chocolate spread with sufficient water to form a thin paste. Cool.
2. Gradually beat in sieved icing sugar to make a stiff pouring consistency.
3. Beat well, adding vanilla essence to taste.

INGREDIENTS
8 oz. icing sugar
**1 tablespoonful
    chocolate spread**
Hot water
Vanilla essence

royal icing

Sieve icing sugar. Place the egg whites and lemon juice in a mixing bowl, gradually mix in icing sugar. Beat well until mixture is white.

Adjust Consistency

If required for *piping* add more sieved icing sugar. The icing should stand in 'peaks'.

If required to *coat* a large cake, add a little more liquid if necessary until a 'spreadable' consistency is obtained.

Use at once, or if required to be left for a short time, cover bowl with a damp cloth.

INGREDIENTS
8 oz. icing sugar
1-1½ egg whites
**¼ teaspoonful lemon
    juice**

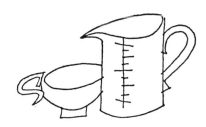

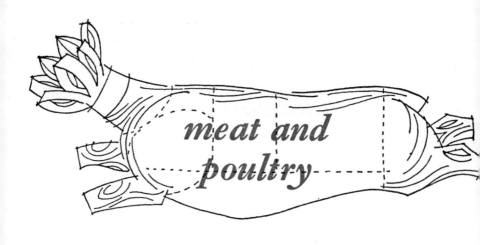

meat and poultry

choice of meat and poultry

Certain joints are more suitable for one cooking method than another, below
is a list to guide you.

Roasting	*Beef*	Topside, Sirloin, Ribs.
	Lamb	Leg, Loin, Best End of Neck, Shoulder, Breast (stuffed).
	Mutton	Leg, Loin, Shoulder.
	Pork	Leg, Loin.
	Veal	Loin, Shoulder.
	Poultry	Spring chicken, Ducks, Duckling, Turkey etc.
	Offal	Heart.
Stewing	*Beef*	Brisket, Shin, Tail.
	Lamb	Breast.
	Mutton	Breast, Scrag End of Neck.
	Veal	Breast, Knuckle, Shoulder.

Boiling	*Beef*	Silverside, Brisket, Shin.
	Mutton	Leg.
	Pork	Ham, Bacon, Belly.
	Poultry	Boiling Fowl.
	Offal	Kidneys, Tongue, Brains, Sweetbreads.
Grilling	*Beef*	Rump and Fillet Steak.
	Lamb	Chops, Leg Cutlets.
	Pork	Chops, Fillets.
	Veal	Fillet.
	Poultry	Chicken joints etc.
	Offal	Kidneys, Liver.

methods of cooking meat and poultry

roasting

The times given below will be found an excellent guide when cooking meat, but slight adjustments may be necessary.

1. Size of joint, a small one takes longer per pound than a large one. (Up to 30 minutes longer for a small joint weighing 2 pounds only.)
2. A short, thick joint takes longer than a thinner one.
3. Boned and rolled joints take longer to cook through than those with the bone left in.
4. Personal preference, e.g. meat well done, medium or rare.
5. Meat with a thick layer of fat takes longer than a lean joint.

If meat is frozen, it should be allowed to thaw before cooking.

Roasting Chart See your Instruction Card for temperature and oven position.

Beef 20–35 minutes per pound + 20 minutes.

Mutton ⎱
Lamb ⎰ 25–35 minutes per pound + 25 minutes.

Pork 35–40 minutes per pound + 35 minutes.

Veal 35–40 minutes per pound + 35 minutes.

Poultry 15–20 minutes per pound + 20 minutes. Cook at the same temperature as for Roast Meat. The temperature may be raised 25°–50° for the final 20/30 minutes cooking time if necessary.

41

Aluminium Foil	When foil is used the cooking time should be increased by approximately one third. To brown and crisp the exterior of the joint remove the foil for the last 20–30 minutes of the cooking period.
Preparation for Roasting	Wipe meat, place in baking tin (fat side uppermost) with a little fat. Amount depends on type of meat, e.g. veal requires more than pork. Lean joints, e.g. veal, also poultry and game may be covered with strips of fat or basted in the usual way.
Roast Turkey	Make up the parsley and thyme stuffing (page 89) increasing the quantity according to the size of the bird (i.e. for 16 lb turkey allow 1 lb breadcrumbs/ 8 ozs suet). Place the stuffing in the neck end of the bird, sausage meat can be placed in the other end. Truss securely and season well. Heat a little dripping and brush over the breast of the bird, the breast can be covered with strips of streaky bacon. Place in the roasting tin and cover the bird with greased grease-proof or foil.

stewing

Stewing is suitable for the cheaper, coarser cuts of meat. Remove fat and cut meat into small even sized pieces, or leave whole as desired.

Flavouring ingredients are usually added, e.g. onion, carrot, turnip, mixed herbs, seasoning. Add liquid. Cover with a tight fitting lid, cook slowly until meat is tender. Never let a stew boil, only an occasional bubble should appear on the surface.

frying

The more expensive cuts of meat are cooked by this method.

Wipe meat, remove surplus fat. Brown each side of the meat at a fairly high temperature, reduce heat and continue cooking at a lower temperature until tender.

grilling

Choose meat as for frying.

Wipe meat and remove surplus fat. Grill.

Meat to be grilled may also be steeped in a Marinade before cooking. This will produce delightfully tasty results.

Grilling timetable (Time depends on personal preference and thickness of food.)

Steak	10–15 minutes.
Kidney	8–10 minutes. (Cut in half, remove skin and core. Soak in salt water for 5 minutes. Dry.)
Lamb chops	10–15 minutes.
Pork chops	15–20 minutes.
Veal chops	10–15 minutes.
Sausages	10–15 minutes.
Liver	7–10 minutes.
Bacon	2–3 minutes (Remove rind).
Gammon	5–10 minutes.

boiling

Wipe meat. Trim, remove bone if necessary, tie into compact shape. Place meat in boiling water, allow to boil for 5 minutes. Reduce heat and simmer for required time.

Fresh meat	20 minutes per pound + 20 minutes.
Salt meat	25 minutes per pound + 25 minutes.
Bacon, Tongue	30 minutes per pound + 30 minutes.
Fowl	1–2½ hours according to age.

43

baked stuffed liver

1. Wash liver and remove skin if necessary, place in dish.
2. Make up stuffing (page 90).
3. Spread stuffing over liver. Remove rind from bacon, arrange to cover liver and stuffing. Add stock. Bake.

INGREDIENTS
¾ lb. liver (sliced)
4 rashers bacon
Sage and onion stuffing
¼ pint stock

beef olives

1. Beat steak, cut into strips, approx. 3″ × 4″. Make up stuffing (page 90). Spread steak with stuffing, roll up and secure with a cocktail stick or tie with coarse cotton. Place meat in dish.
2. Blend flour with a little of the measured stock, add remainder, pour into dish. Cover with foil. Bake.
   To serve, remove cocktail sticks or cotton from meat, place on a serving dish. Season sauce and pour over meat.

INGREDIENTS
¾ lb. steak (cut ¼″ thick in slices)
Sage and onion stuffing
½ pint stock
Seasoning
2 teaspoonfuls flour

chicken casserole

1. Blend flour with a little of the stock, add remainder.
2. Add seasoning, mixed herbs, tomato purée and onion.
3. Place chicken joints in dish, add stock. Cover with foil. Bake.
4. Place chicken on serving dish. Strain sauce and pour over.

INGREDIENTS
4 joints chicken
½-¾ pint stock
1 small onion (finely chopped)
2 tablespoonfuls tomato purée
2 teaspoonfuls flour
Pinch mixed herbs
Seasoning

chicken maryland

1. Make up coating batter (page 16).
2. Remove bone from thigh joint and drumsticks. Season meat and dip in batter. Fry in deep fat. Drain.
3. Cut bananas lengthwise and across, sprinkle with flour and dip in batter. Fry in deep fat. Drain.

Serve with grilled tomatoes, bacon rolls (page 51), Brown Sauce and sweet corn.

INGREDIENTS
4 chicken joints (cooked)
2 bananas
Coating batter
Seasoning

Garnish
4 tomatoes
4 rashers bacon
Sweet corn
Brown sauce

cornish pasties

1. Make up pastry (page 54). Divide into 6 equal portions, roll each into a circle 7" in diameter.
2. Cut meat into small pieces, mix with prepared onion and potato. Add seasoning and water, mix well together.
3. Divide filling into 6 equal portions, place on rolled pastry. Moisten edges of pastry and pinch together at top. Place on baking trays. Brush with beaten egg. Bake.

Other flavourings may be used with or in place of onion, e.g. grated carrot, mixed herbs, parsley, etc.

INGREDIENTS
16 oz. shortcrust pastry
¾ lb. steak
6 oz. onions (finely chopped)
8 oz. potatoes (finely chopped)
Beaten egg
Seasoning
2 tablespoonfuls water

curried meat

Make up Curry Sauce (page 67). Add meat to sauce, reheat just before serving. Serve with plain boiled rice.

INGREDIENTS
¾ lb. diced cooked meat
¾ pint curry sauce

NOTE
Place over a very gentle heat and take care not to allow the mixture to boil.

hot pot

1. Cut steak into small pieces, removing fat. Wash and skin kidney, soak in salt water for 5 minutes, dice. Slice carrots, skin and quarter tomatoes.
2. Melt dripping in pan and fry onion, carrot and meat until lightly browned.
3. Place steak, kidney, tomatoes, onion, carrot, seasoning and stock in a dish and cover. Cook.
4. When cooked, strain off liquor. Arrange meat etc., on a serving dish.
5. Blend flour with a little of the stock, add remainder. Bring to the boil, stirring continually, cook for 3 minutes. Pour over meat and vegetables.

INGREDIENTS
1 lb. lean stewing steak
2 oz. kidney
1 onion (finely chopped)
2 carrots
2 tomatoes
½ oz. dripping
1 oz. flour
½ pint stock
Seasoning

meat pie (flaky pastry)

Make up pastry (page 53). Shape as for Shortcrust Fruit Pie (page 61). Brush with beaten egg before baking.

INGREDIENTS
8 oz. flaky pastry
1½ lb. cooked meat
Gravy
Beaten egg

NOTE
Use a pie funnel if necessary.

meat pie (shortcrust)

Make up pastry (page 54). Shape as for Shortcrust Fruit Pie (page 61).

INGREDIENTS
12 oz. shortcrust pastry
1½ lb. cooked meat
Gravy

NOTE
Use a pie funnel if necessary.

meat pie (plate)

Make up pastry (page 54). Shape as for Fruit Pie (Plate) (page 62).

INGREDIENTS
14 oz. shortcrust pastry
Cooked meat
Gravy

meat pudding

1. Wash and skin kidney, soak in cold salt water for 5 minutes. Remove fat from beef, wipe. Dice meat and kidney, toss in seasoned flour.
2. Make up pastry (page 54).
3. Grease pudding basin. Roll out ⅔ of pastry and line basin. Fill with prepared beef and kidney. Add water.
4. Roll out remaining pastry to form a lid. Moisten edge and press onto lining pastry.
5. Cover with a piece of greased greaseproof paper and a pudding cloth. Secure.
6. Place in a saucepan (with a tight fitting lid) containing enough water to come half way up the basin. Cook for the required time.

When adding water to maintain level, it must be boiling.

INGREDIENTS
6 oz. suet crust pastry
1 lb. stewing beef
4 oz. kidney
3 tablespoonfuls water
1 tablespoonful seasoned flour

SIZE OF BASIN
1½ pint

COOKING TIME
3-4 hours

mock roast

1. Melt margarine, add flour and cook together for a few minutes over a low heat, stirring all the time.
2. Remove pan from heat, add stock, a little at a time, blending well, to form a smooth paste. Add remaining stock.
3. Bring mixture to boil, cook for 3-5 minutes, continue to stir. Add herbs, seasoning and meat extract.
4. Place meat in dish, pour over sauce. Cover dish with foil. Bake.

INGREDIENTS
4 thick slices cooked beef or lamb
1 oz. margarine
1 oz. flour
½ pint stock
Seasoning
Pinch mixed herbs
1 teaspoonful meat extract

47

monday special

1. Skin and chop tomatoes. Melt margarine in a saucepan, add onion, tomatoes, finely chopped mushrooms and seasoning. Fry gently until onion and mushrooms are cooked.
2. Blend flour with a little of the measured stock, stir in remainder. Add this mixture to the fried ingredients, bring to the boil, stirring continually. Cook for 5 minutes.
3. Add meat to sauce, reheat just before serving.

INGREDIENTS

Sliced cold beef or lamb
1 large onion (finely chopped)
1 oz. margarine
1 oz. flour
½ pint stock
3 tomatoes
2 oz. mushrooms
Seasoning

NOTE
Place over a very gentle heat and take care not to allow the mixture to boil.

rissoles

1. Melt fat and fry onion until cooked.
2. Add flour and cook together for a few minutes over a low heat, stirring all the time.
3. Remove pan from heat, add stock, a little at a time. Blend well.
4. Bring mixture to the boil, cook for 3–5 minutes, continue to stir. Remove from heat.
5. Add meat and season well with salt, pepper and Worcester sauce. Turn out onto a plate and cool.
6. When cool place on a floured board and divide into 6. Shape each portion into a round flat cake.
7. Coat with flour, egg and raspings. Fry in hot fat until heated through. Serve with Tomato Sauce.

INGREDIENTS

1 lb. cooked meat (minced)
1 oz. lard
1 oz. flour
1 medium onion (finely chopped)
¼ pint stock
Seasoning
Worcester sauce

Coating
Flour, beaten egg, raspings

savoury chicken

1. Place the stock, finely chopped onion, chopped bacon, skinned chopped tomato and seasoning into a large saucepan.
2. Place strips of lemon rind and mace in a piece of muslin and tie. Place in the saucepan.
3. Bring to the boil, add chicken, cover with a lid and simmer for 35 minutes.
4. Add rice, continue to cook for a further 30–45 minutes when rice should be cooked and stock absorbed. Remove muslin, serve.

INGREDIENTS
4 tomatoes
4 pieces chicken (fresh or thawed)
2 streaky rashers
1 onion
Rind of ¼ lemon
Blade mace
Seasoning
4 oz. Patna rice
¾ pint stock

shepherds pie

1. Cook chopped onion in stock until tender, add Worcester sauce, breadcrumbs, nutmeg, seasoning and meat. Mix thoroughly and place in greased dish.
2. Mash potato, add margarine and egg. Beat well and place on top of meat, smooth over and bake.

INGREDIENTS
¾ lb. minced cooked meat
1 small onion (finely chopped)
½ pint stock
Seasoning
1-2 tablespoonfuls Worcester sauce
1 tablespoonful breadcrumbs
Pinch grated nutmeg
1 lb. cooked potato
½ oz. margarine
½ egg

stuffed hearts

1. Soak hearts in cold salt water, clean thoroughly. Remove pipes and trim.
2. Make up stuffing (page 90). Fill hearts with stuffing, secure top with a small skewer.
3. Place upright in dish, add stock. Cover with foil. Bake.
4. To serve, arrange hearts in a dish. Drain some fat from stock. Blend flour with a little stock, add remainder. Bring to the boil, stirring continually, cook for 3 minutes. Pour over hearts.

INGREDIENTS
4 sheep's hearts
Sage and onion stuffing
½ pint stock
Seasoning
1 teaspoonful flour

stuffed pork chops

1. Prepare chops, place in dish. Season.
2. Make up stuffing (page 90). Spread stuffing over chops. Dot with lard, cover with foil, do not seal. Bake.
Serve with Apple Sauce.
A layer of finely chopped onions may be placed under chops.

INGREDIENTS
4 pork chops
Sage and onion stuffing
1 oz. lard
Seasoning

veal and ham patties

1. Make up pastry (page 53). Roll out to a thickness of $\frac{1}{8}''-\frac{1}{4}''$. Using a $2\frac{1}{2}''$ cutter, cut out 12 lids.
2. Roll remainder of pastry wafer thin and cut 12 'bases' using a 3" cutter.
3. Mix together ham, veal, seasoning, thyme, lemon rind, parsley and water.
4. Line patty tins with pastry, fill with meat mixture and cover. Brush with beaten egg. Bake.

INGREDIENTS
8 oz. flaky pastry
6 oz. lean veal (finely diced)
2 oz. ham (finely diced)
2 tablespoonfuls water
Rind of ¼ lemon (finely grated)
½ teaspoonful chopped parsley
Pinch thyme
Seasoning
Beaten egg

veal fricassee

1. Simmer veal, onion, mixed herbs, seasoning and water together for 1 hour or until veal is tender.
2. Strain off liquid and make up to ½ pint with milk. Make a White Sauce (page 68) using this liquid in place of milk.
3. Season with lemon juice, salt and pepper. Add onions and veal. Reheat.
   Serve garnished with cooked mushroom slices, bacon rolls, and lemon slices.

Bacon Rolls. Halve rashers of streaky bacon. Remove rind and roll up. Grill.

INGREDIENTS
¾ **lb. stewing veal (diced)**
1 onion (finely chopped)
½ **pint water**
2 teaspoonfuls lemon juice
Seasoning
Pinch mixed herbs
½ **pint White Sauce**

Garnish
Mushrooms
Bacon rolls
Lemon

mixing

Rubbing in   See cake section (page 21).

Kneading   Pastry is kneaded to make a smooth and silky mixture. The mixture is brought from the outside to the centre (using the finger tips), pressing gently into a smooth ball.

Rolling out   Dredge board with flour, roll lightly but do not stretch pastry.

ingredients

Water   Add water very carefully, if too much is added, the pastry is difficult to shape and hard when cooked. Use ice cold water for best results. Mix in with a knife until mixture begins to bind together. Press together with the fingertips.

Fat   Use hard margarine and lard for Flaky Pastry. Use finely chopped suet for Suet Crust Pastry.

Weigh or measure all ingredients very carefully.

NOTE   *If pastry is to be stored before use, always wrap well in waxed paper to prevent a dry skin forming. Remember tins for pastry need no preparation.*

flan case

To bake blind   Roll pastry into a circle, 1″ larger than the tin. Place pastry in the tin, using the rolling pin to transport pastry to prevent stretching, ease in. Trim edges. Mould pastry against side of tin, with fingers. Prick base lightly, place a greaseproof paper disc in the base and cover with a few beans.

About 5 minutes before end of cooking time, remove paper and beans, return flan case to the oven for remainder of time to dry out the base.

flaky pastry

1. Mix margarine and lard together, divide into 4 portions.
2. Sieve flour and salt, rub in one portion of fat. Add lemon juice and sufficient water to form a soft dough. Knead.
3. Roll out into an oblong strip approx. 5″ × 15″. Add second portion of fat by spreading in 'dots' over ⅔ of pastry. Fold in three, with the portion of pastry without fat in the centre.
4. Turn pastry so that the 'open side' is to the right, roll out and add third portion of fat as before.
5. Repeat, using final portion of fat. It may be necessary to leave pastry between each rolling in a cool place to allow fat to become firm. If this is done, wrap well or a dry skin will form.
6. Leave in a cool place before using as required.

INGREDIENTS

8 oz. plain flour
3 oz. margarine
3 oz. lard
Pinch salt
2 teaspoonfuls lemon juice
Cold water

NOTE
When using pastry scraps or re-rolling, place trimmings on top of each other and then re-roll, do not gather together.

53

flan pastry

1. Sieve flour, sugar and salt together. Make a well in the centre, drop in egg and margarine.
2. Knead mixture together until a soft pliable dough is formed. Use as required.

INGREDIENTS
12 oz. plain flour
8 oz. margarine
2 oz. caster sugar
1 egg
Pinch salt

shortcrust pastry

1. Sieve flour and salt into a mixing bowl.
2. Rub in fat.
3. Mix to a stiff dough, using cold water. Turn out onto a floured board and knead lightly. Use as required.

INGREDIENTS
8 oz. plain flour
2 oz. margarine
2 oz. lard
Pinch salt
Cold water

suet crust pastry

1. Sieve flour and salt, stir in chopped suet.
2. Mix to a soft dough, using cold water. Turn out onto a floured board and knead lightly. Use as required.

INGREDIENTS
8 oz. self raising flour
4 oz. suet
Pinch salt
Cold water

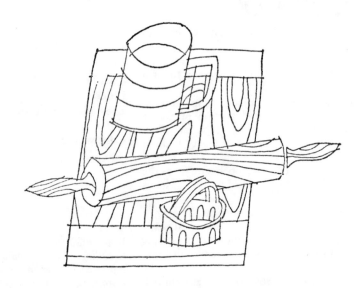

puddings

apple amber

1. Make up pastry (page 54). Roll out and line dish, pinch up edges and bake blind (page 53).
2. Cut up apples and stew with a little water until soft. Sieve and sweeten, add lemon rind.
3. Beat egg yolks and add to apples.
4. When pastry is cooked, remove from oven and cool slightly. Place apple mixture on pastry.
5. Whisk egg whites until stiff, add half sugar and continue beating. Fold in remaining sugar. Use to cover apple mixture. Bake.

INGREDIENTS
8 oz. shortcrust pastry

Filling
1 lb. cooking apples
Rind of ½ lemon (finely grated)
2 egg yolks
Water
Sugar to taste

Meringue
2 egg whites
3 oz. caster sugar

apple charlotte

1. Mix together breadcrumbs, suet, and sugar.
2. Grease dish and coat sides with crumb mixture.
3. Prepare apples and sultanas. Mix with lemon rind.
4. Place crumb and apple mixture in layers, starting and finishing with a layer of crumbs. Bake.

INGREDIENTS
6 oz. white breadcrumbs
3 oz. suet
3 oz. caster sugar
1 lb. apples
4 oz. sultanas
Rind of 1 lemon (finely grated)

apple dumplings

1. Make up pastry (page 54). Cut into 4 equal portions and roll out into circles.
2. Peel and core apples, place on pastry.
3. Fill centre of apples with sugar, damp edges of pastry and mould over apples. Place (join downwards) on baking tray.
4. Using a skewer, make a few incisions in pastry to let steam escape during cooking. Bake.

INGREDIENTS
8 oz. shortcrust pastry
4 medium size apples
Sugar

NOTE
These dumplings may be filled with dried fruit, sugar and spice in place of sugar only.

apple pudding

1. Make up pastry (page 54).
2. Grease pudding basin. Roll out ⅔ pastry and line basin. Fill with prepared apples, add cloves, sugar and water.
3. Roll out remaining pastry to form a lid. Moisten edge and press onto lining pastry.
4. Cover with a piece of greased greaseproof paper and pudding cloth. Secure.
5. Place in a suacepan (with a tight fitting lid) containing enough boiling water to come half way up the basin. Cook for the required time.
When adding water to maintain level, it must be boiling.

INGREDIENTS
6 oz. suet crust pastry
1 lb. cooking apples
4 cloves
3 tablespoonfuls water
3 oz. sugar

SIZE OF BASIN
1½ pint

COOKING TIME
2 hours approx.

NOTE
Any fruit may be used in place of apples.

baked custard

1. Mix milk with sugar, heat until dissolved. Pour onto lightly beaten eggs. Mix in vanilla essence.
2. Strain into lightly greased dish, sprinkle with grated nutmeg. Bake.

INGREDIENTS
3 eggs
1 oz. sugar
1 pint milk
Vanilla essence
Nutmeg

baked pudding

1. Grease dish.
2. Sieve flour and salt, rub in fat. Add sugar.
3. Stir in lightly beaten egg and enough milk to make a fairly stiff mixture.
4. Place in prepared dish. Bake. Serve with Jam Sauce.

INGREDIENTS
8 oz. self raising flour
4 oz. margarine
4 oz. caster sugar
⅛–¼ pint milk
1 egg
Pinch salt

coconut pudding

Make up mixture as for previous recipe, adding most of coconut with sugar. The remainder may be sprinkled on top for decoration. Serve with Jam Sauce.

INGREDIENTS
2 oz. desiccated coconut

ginger pudding

Make up mixture as for Baked Pudding, sieving ground ginger with flour and salt. Add chopped ginger with syrup. Serve with warmed syrup.

INGREDIENTS
1 teaspoonful ground ginger
2 oz. coarsely chopped crystallised ginger

lemon pudding

Make up mixture as for Baked Pudding, adding lemon rind with egg. Serve with warmed lemon cheese.

INGREDIENTS
Rind of 1 lemon (finely grated)

marmalade pudding

Make up mixture as for Baked Pudding. Before placing mixture in dish, spread a little marmalade over base of dish. Serve with warmed marmalade.

INGREDIENTS
Marmalade

fruit pudding

Make up mixture as for Baked Pudding, adding mixed fruit with sugar. Serve with Custard Sauce.

INGREDIENTS
8 oz. mixed dried fruit

baked stuffed apples

1. Core apples and score round centre with knife.
2. Mix fruit, sugar, butter and spice together and use to stuff centre of apple.
3. Place stuffed apples in baking tin with a little water and bake.

INGREDIENTS
4 medium size apples
Water

Filling
2 oz. mixed dried fruit
2 oz. sugar
1 oz. butter
Pinch mixed spice

bread and butter pudding

1. Grease dish and line with 3 slices of bread and butter. Sprinkle with currants, sugar and grated nutmeg.
2. Cover with remaining bread and butter.
3. Beat eggs and milk. Pour over the pudding. Leave to stand 30 minutes before cooking.
4. Sprinkle with grated nutmeg. Bake.

INGREDIENTS
1 pint milk
1 oz. sugar
2 eggs
1 oz. currants
6 small slices bread and butter
Nutmeg

casserole fruit

1. Leave fruit to soak in cold water overnight.
2. Drain. Place in dish with sugar, water and lemon rind. Cover with lid or foil. Bake.
3. When cooked remove lemon rind. Serve with cream.

INGREDIENTS
4 oz. dried apricots
4 oz. dried prunes
1-2 oz. sugar
$\frac{1}{4}$-$\frac{1}{2}$ pint water
Rind of $\frac{1}{2}$ lemon (cut into strips)

crème caramel

1. *Caramel.* Place sugar and water in a small saucepan. Leave until sugar is dissolved.
2. Bring to boil. Allow to boil quickly (do not stir) until mixture turns pale brown. Remove at once.
3. Pour caramel into greased basin. Move gently until base and sides are coated. Leave until quite cold.
4. *Crème.* Beat eggs, stir into milk. Add sugar and vanilla essence.
5. Pour into prepared basin. Cover with foil or greased greaseproof paper. Steam for the required time.

To serve, run a knife round sides of basin and invert onto serving dish.

INGREDIENTS
$\frac{1}{2}$ pint milk
3 eggs
1 oz. caster sugar
$\frac{1}{2}$ teaspoonful vanilla essence

Caramel
4 oz. sugar
$\frac{1}{4}$ pint water

SIZE OF BASIN
1-1$\frac{1}{4}$ pint

COOKING TIME
30-40 minutes

christmas pudding

1. Butter basins.
2. Sieve flour, salt, mixed spice, ground ginger, cinnamon and grated nutmeg together.
3. Add breadcrumbs, brown sugar, chopped suet, currants, raisins, sultanas, mixed peel, ground almonds and lemon rind.
4. Beat eggs with almond essence, add to mixture.
5. Add liquid and mix very thoroughly.
6. Pour into prepared basins.
7. Cover with a piece of greased greaseproof paper and a pudding cloth. Secure.
8. Place in a saucepan (with a tight fitting lid) containing enough water to come half way up the basin. Cook for the required time. When adding water to maintain level, it must be boiling. When cooked, cover with a new piece of paper and store until required. Reheat by the same method as cooking.

INGREDIENTS
4 oz. self raising flour
8 oz. fresh white breadcrumbs
8 oz. brown sugar
8 oz. chopped suet
8 oz. currants
8 oz. raisins
8 oz. sultanas
4 oz. mixed peel
1 oz. ground almonds
4 eggs
Rind of 1 lemon (finely grated)
1 teaspoonful almond essence
½ teaspoonful ground ginger
½ teaspoonful mixed spice
½ teaspoonful cinnamon
Pinch salt
Pinch grated nutmeg
½ pint milk or Barley wine

SIZE OF BASIN
2-1½ pint

COOKING TIME
8 hours approx.

rice pudding

1. Place rice, milk and sugar in dish.
2. Dot with margarine and sprinkle with grated nutmeg. Bake.

INGREDIENTS
1 pint milk
1 oz. sugar
1 oz. margarine
2 oz. rice
Nutmeg

egg custard flan

1. Make up pastry (page 54). Roll out to a thickness of $\frac{1}{8}"-\frac{1}{4}"$. Line sandwich tin and bake blind (page 53).
2. Beat eggs, add milk and sugar. Place in a saucepan and *warm* only, over a gentle heat.
3. When flan is cool, spread jam over base, pour in warmed filling. Sprinkle with grated nutmeg. Bake at once.

INGREDIENTS
4 oz. flan pastry

Filling
Jam
$\frac{1}{4}$ pint milk
2 eggs
Sugar to taste
Nutmeg

fruit fritters

1. Make up Coating Batter (page 16).
2. Dry fruit and dip in batter to coat evenly. Fry in deep fat. Drain.
3. Sprinkle with caster sugar and serve very hot.

INGREDIENTS
Sliced apple, soaked in lemon juice and sugar
Sliced banana
Orange segments
Pieces of pineapple
Coating batter
Caster sugar

fruit pie (shortcrust)

1. Make up pastry (page 54).
2. Prepare fruit and place in dish with 2-4 tablespoonfuls water (according to fruit) and sugar.
3. Roll out the pastry a little larger than the dish, cut off a strip about $\frac{1}{2}"$ wide. Damp and press this strip of pastry onto the edge of dish, damp again and cover with the remaining pastry. Trim and decorate edges. Bake.

INGREDIENTS
12 oz. shortcrust pastry
2 lb. fruit
Sugar to taste
Water

NOTE
Use a pie funnel if necessary.

fruit pie (plate)

1. Make up pastry (page 54). Cut in half, line plate with one portion and roll remaining portion to cover.
2. Prepare apples, slice. Arrange on lined plate, sprinkle with sugar and add flavouring. Damp edges of pastry, cover and seal edge by pinching up. Make a small incision in top to allow steam to escape. Bake.

INGREDIENTS
14 oz. shortcrust pastry
1-1½ lb. cooking apples
Sugar to taste
Cloves or lemon rind

NOTE
Any fruit may be used in place of apples, tinned or fresh.

mincemeat pie

Make up as for previous recipe, substituting mincemeat for apples, sugar and flavouring.

INGREDIENTS
Mincemeat

lemon meringue pie

1. Make up pastry (page 54). Roll out and line tin. Bake blind (page 53).
2. Place sugar, butter, water, lemon juice and rind in a saucepan. Heat, stirring until the sugar has dissolved. Cool.
3. Blend cornflour with a little milk, add remainder. Stir into heated mixture and bring to the boil. Continue to stir until the mixture thickens. Cool slightly.
4. Beat egg yolks and add the thickened mixture. Pour into pastry case.
5. Whisk egg whites until stiff, add half sugar and continue beating. Fold in remaining sugar. Use to cover lemon mixture. Bake.

INGREDIENTS
10 oz. shortcrust pastry

Filling
2½ oz. caster sugar
1½ oz. butter
3 egg yolks
1 oz. cornflour
¼ pint water
¼ pint milk
2 lemons. Juice and finely grated rind

Meringue
3 egg whites
4 oz. caster sugar

mince pies

1. Make up pastry (page 53). Roll out to a thickness of $\frac{1}{8}"-\frac{1}{4}"$. Using a $2\frac{1}{2}"$ cutter, cut out 16 'lids'.
2. Roll remainder of pastry wafer thin and cut 16 'bases' using a $3"$ cutter.
3. Line patty tins with pastry, fill with mincemeat and cover. Bake. When cold, dredge with icing sugar.

INGREDIENTS
8 oz. flaky pastry
8-12 oz. mincemeat

pastry fruit flan

1. Make up pastry (page 54).
2. Roll out to $\frac{1}{8}"-\frac{1}{4}"$ thickness. Line sandwich tin and bake blind (page 53). When cold, fill with fruit and cover with Arrowroot Glaze (page 66).

INGREDIENTS
6 oz. flan pastry
Fruit
Arrowroot Glaze

pineapple upside-down pudding

1. Grease tin.
2. Melt demerara sugar, butter and lemon juice. Boil till thick.
3. Arrange pineapple and cherries in base of tin. Carefully pour over boiled mixture. Leave to set.
4. Sieve flour and salt.
5. Separate egg yolks from whites. Beat yolks with sugar, add water and continue to beat until mixture is fairly stiff. Mix in lemon rind.
6. Fold in flour, add more water if necessary to make a soft mixture.
7. Whisk egg whites until stiff. Fold into mixture, place in tin. Bake.
8. When cooked, run a knife round edge of tin, invert on serving dish. Leave for 5 minutes. Remove tin. Serve.

INGREDIENTS
1 small tin pineapple rings
3-4 glacé cherries
4 oz. demerara sugar
3 tablespoonfuls lemon juice
1 oz. butter
4 oz. self raising flour
5 oz. caster sugar
2 eggs
Rind of 1 lemon (finely grated)
2-3 tablespoonfuls tepid water
Pinch salt

sponge fruit flan

Prepare tin as for Sponge Sandwich. Make up mixture as for Swiss Roll (page 30). Bake. When flan is cold, arrange fruit in centre. Make Arrowroot Glaze (page 66). Pour over fruit.

INGREDIENTS
Swiss roll mixture
Fruit
Arrowroot glaze

steamed pudding

Make up mixture as for Baked Pudding (page 57). Place mixture in a greased basin. Cover with a piece of greased greaseproof paper and a pudding cloth. Secure. Place in a saucepan with a tight fitting lid containing enough water to come half way up the basin, cook for the required time.

When adding water to maintain this level, it must be boiling.

Variations as for Baked Pudding, serve with appropriate sauce.

INGREDIENTS
Baked pudding mixture

SIZE OF BASIN
1½ pint

COOKING TIME
1½ hours

syrup tart

1. Make up pastry (page 54). Line plate, re-roll trimmings, cut into strips ½″ wide for decoration.

   Mix breadcrumbs and lemon rind with syrup. Pour filling into lined plate. Place strips of pastry lattice fashion over filling. Pinch up edges. Bake.

INGREDIENTS
8 oz. shortcrust pastry

Filling
12 oz. golden syrup
2 oz. white breadcrumbs
Rind of ½ lemon (finely grated)

jam tart

Make up tart as for previous recipe, using jam only for filling.

When using plum jam, the flavour is improved if a little ground ginger is mixed with the jam before placing in lined plate.

INGREDIENTS

Jam

lemon cheese tart

Make up as for Syrup Tart, using lemon cheese only for filling.

INGREDIENTS

Lemon cheese

sauces & glazes

apple sauce

1. Prepare apples, cook over a gentle heat with margarine, sugar and water.
2. When cooked, add lemon juice and beat well or sieve. Reheat and use as desired.

INGREDIENTS
1 lb. cooking apples
½ oz. margarine
Sugar to taste
Few drops lemon juice
Water

arrowroot glaze

1. Blend arrowroot with a little of the measured fruit juice. Bring remainder to the boil and pour over blended arrowroot.
2. Add sugar. Place mixture in a small saucepan and boil for a few minutes, stirring all the time. Colour. Use as desired.

INGREDIENTS
¼ pint fruit juice
2 heaped teaspoonfuls arrowroot
Sugar to taste
Colouring

bread sauce

1. Stick the cloves in the onion, place in milk with peppercorns, butter and mace. Cook over a gentle heat for about 30 minutes.
2. Strain milk and pour over breadcrumbs. Beat.
3. Season to taste. Stand aside until required. Reheat.

INGREDIENTS
2 oz. breadcrumbs
½ pint milk
Seasoning
1 medium onion
½ oz. butter
3 cloves
6 peppercorns
½ blade mace

brown sauce

1. Prepare vegetables (if using large onions and old carrots chop well or grate, this will reduce cooking time). Melt margarine, fry vegetables lightly.
2. Add stock and seasoning, bring to the boil and cook gently for 30 minutes or until vegetables are tender. Cool.
3. Blend flour with a little water, add to mixture.
4. Bring to the boil, stirring continually. Cook for 3 minutes. Sieve, season and reheat. Add gravy browning to colour.

INGREDIENTS
1 onion
1 carrot
½ pint stock
Seasoning
½ oz. margarine
½ oz. flour
Gravy browning

curry sauce

1. Melt margarine and fry onion until lightly cooked.
2. Add flour and curry powder and cook for 2-3 minutes.
3. Pour in stock, a little at a time, blending well to form a smooth paste. Add remainder of stock. Bring to boil.
4. Add apple and sultanas, simmer until apple is cooked.
5. Stir in sugar, seasoning and lemon juice.

INGREDIENTS
2 oz. margarine
1 onion (finely chopped)
1 oz. flour
1 level tablespoonful curry powder
¾ pint stock
2 oz. sultanas
1 apple (sliced)
2 teaspoonfuls lemon juice
Seasoning
½ teaspoonful caster sugar

jam sauce

1. Blend arrowroot with a little of the measured water, bring the remainder to the boil and pour over blended arrowroot.
2. Add jam and lemon juice.
3. Place mixture in a small saucepan and boil for a few minutes, stirring all the time. Use as desired.

INGREDIENTS
2 tablespoonfuls jam
¼ pint water (liberal)
2 teaspoonfuls lemon juice
1 teaspoonful arrowroot

fruit sauce

Make as for Jam Sauce (page 67) using fruit juice in place of water and omitting jam.

INGREDIENTS
Fruit juice

mint sauce

1. Pour boiling water over prepared mint, add sugar. Cool.
2. Add salt and vinegar.

INGREDIENTS
¼ **pint vinegar**
4 **heaped tablespoonfuls finely chopped mint**
2 **tablespoonfuls boiling water**
1 **dessertspoonful sugar**
Pinch salt

white sauce

1. Melt margarine, add flour and cook together for a few minutes over a low heat, stirring all the time.
2. Remove pan from heat, add milk, a little at a time, blending well, to form a smooth paste. Add remaining milk.
3. Bring mixture to boil, cook for 3–5 minutes, continue to stir. Season.

INGREDIENTS
1 **oz. flour**
1 **oz. margarine or butter**
½ **pint milk**
Seasoning

cheese sauce

Make up as for White Sauce, add 1 tablespoonful finely grated cheese (Parmesan or strong). Do not reheat.

anchovy sauce

Make up as for White Sauce, add 1 teaspoonful anchovy essence and a few drops of lemon juice. Reheat.

onion sauce

Make up as for White Sauce, add 1 large cooked onion (finely chopped). Reheat. Onion liquor may be used in place of some milk.

parsley sauce

Make up as for White Sauce, add 1 dessertspoonful finely chopped parsley. Reheat. Beat in knob of butter.

shrimp sauce

Make up for White Sauce, add a few drops of lemon juice and prepared shrimps. A little anchovy essence may be added. Reheat.

tomato sauce

1. Place tomatoes, herbs, onion, water, meat extract, bacon and seasoning together in a saucepan. Bring to the boil and cook over a gentle heat for 20–30 minutes, until onion is cooked.
2. Blend flour with a little water, add to mixture.
3. Bring to the boil, stirring continually. Cook for 3 minutes. Sieve, season and reheat.

INGREDIENTS
12 oz. tomatoes
Pinch mixed herbs
1 onion (finely chopped)
½ pint water
2 teaspoonfuls meat extract
1 rasher bacon (chopped)
Seasoning
2 teaspoonfuls flour

savouries

egg and bacon flan

1. Make up pastry (page 54). Roll out to $\frac{1}{8}''-\frac{1}{4}''$ thickness. Line sandwich tin and bake blind (page 53).
2. Beat eggs, milk, onion and seasoning together, stir in bacon. Place in a saucepan and *warm* only over a gentle heat.
3. When flan case is cool, pour in filling. Bake at once. Decorate with cooked mushrooms.

INGREDIENTS
4 oz. shortcrust pastry

Filling
$\frac{1}{4}$ pint milk
2 eggs
2 rashers bacon (chopped)
1 teaspoonful onion (finely chopped)
Seasoning

Garnish
Mushrooms

sausage rolls

1. Make up pastry (page 53). Roll out into an oblong about 20″ × 10″. Cut into two pieces lengthwise.
2. Halve sausage meat and roll each piece into a long strip about 20″ long. Place on pastry.
3. Damp edge of pastry, fold over sausage meat and seal edges, brush with beaten egg. Cut each strip into 6 equal portions. Place on a baking tray. Make two cuts in the top of each roll. Bake.

INGREDIENTS
8 oz. flaky pastry
1 lb. sausage meat
Beaten egg

savoury rice

1. Place stock in a 6″ saucepan, bring to the boil, add rice. Cover with a lid and simmer for 10–15 minutes. Remove from heat.
2. Remove lid, leave to stand for 15 minutes, when the liquid should be absorbed. Reheat.

INGREDIENTS
4 oz. Patna rice
$\frac{3}{4}$ pint stock

71

fried rice

1. Melt fat, add onion, bacon and mushrooms. Fry gently until cooked. Add rice, cook for about 10 minutes.
2. Add skinned, chopped tomatoes, sliced olives, purée and Soy Sauce. Mix well.
3. Pour beaten egg over the rice, do not stir. Cook very slowly until the egg has set. Serve at once.

INGREDIENTS
8 oz. cooked rice
2 small onions (finely chopped)
Stuffed olives
1-2 dessertspoonfuls Soy Sauce
2 oz. mushrooms (finely chopped)
2 rashers bacon (finely chopped)
2 eggs
1 oz. lard
2 tomatoes
1 teaspoonful tomato purée
Seasoning

yarmouth fingers

1. Make up pastry (page 54). Roll out into 2 strips 5" × 6".
2. Mash kippers. Spread on 1 strip of pastry to within 1" of edges.
3. Damp edges and cover with remaining strip. Seal and pinch up. Cut into 6 fingers. Brush with beaten egg. Bake.

These can also be made using sardines in place of kipper. Remove excess oil from 1 tin. Mash sardines, removing tails and backbones. Shape as above.

INGREDIENTS
4 oz. shortcrust pastry
1 small pair kippers (filleted)
Beaten egg

welsh rarebit

1. Melt butter. Add cheese, milk, mustard, salt and pepper.
2. Heat gently until cheese has melted. Pour onto prepared toast.
3. Place under grill to brown. Serve immediately.

INGREDIENTS
2 large slices hot buttered toast
4 oz. cheese (grated)
1 oz. butter
1 tablespoonful milk
Pinch dry mustard, salt, pepper

scones

Scone mixtures contain very little fat, therefore become stale very quickly. Scones are best eaten hot or within a day of being baked.

dropped scones

1. Sieve flour, salt, cream of tartar, and bicarbonate of soda.
2. Rub in margarine. Stir in sugar.
3. Add lightly beaten egg and most of milk. Mix to a soft batter, adding rest of milk if necessary. Beat well.
4. Heat a girdle or heavy frying pan and grease it lightly with a piece of suet.
5. Pour spoonfuls of the batter on to the girdle. Cook the scones, turning when bubbles appear on uncooked side.
6. Cool between the folds of a teacloth on a cake rack.
   Serve at once with butter. Approx. 15 scones.

INGREDIENTS
4 oz. plain flour
1 oz. margarine
1 oz. caster sugar
½ egg
¼ pint milk
½ level teaspoonful bicarbonate of soda
1 level teaspoonful cream of tartar
Pinch salt

scones

1. Sieve flour, salt and baking powder. Rub in margarine.
2. Stir in sugar.
3. Add liquid and work mixture into a soft dough.
4. Roll out to ½" thick. Using a 2" cutter, cut into small scones (approx. 18). Place on baking tray. Bake.

INGREDIENTS
12 oz. self raising flour
3 oz. margarine
1 oz. caster sugar
¼ pint milk or milk and water mixed
1 level teaspoonful baking powder
Pinch salt

cheese scones

Make up mixture as for Scones (page 74), omit sugar. Sieve salt, pepper, mustard and flour together. Add cheese to rubbed in mixture.

INGREDIENTS
4 oz. cheese (finely grated)
½ level teaspoonful salt, pepper and dry mustard

mixed fruit scones

Make up mixture as for Scones (page 74). Add fruit and peel to rubbed in mixture.

INGREDIENTS
3 oz. mixed dried fruit
1 oz. mixed peel

date scones

Make up mixture as for Scones (page 74). Add dates to rubbed in mixture.

INGREDIENTS
4 oz. coarsely chopped dates

walnut and coffee scones

Make up mixture as for Scones (page 74). Add nuts with sugar. Mix coffee essence to liquid before adding to rubbed in mixture.

INGREDIENTS
4 oz. coarsely chopped walnuts
1 tablespoonful coffee essence

75

scone round

Make up mixture as for Scones (page 74).
Roll out into a circle 7″ in diameter and place in
the tin. Mark into 8 sections. Bake.

NOTE
This Scone Round can be flavoured as for small
scones, using ½ quantity flavouring ingredients
(page 75).

INGREDIENTS
6 oz. self raising flour
1½ oz. margarine
½ oz. caster sugar
⅛ pint milk or milk and
    water mixed
½ level teaspoonful
    baking powder
Pinch salt

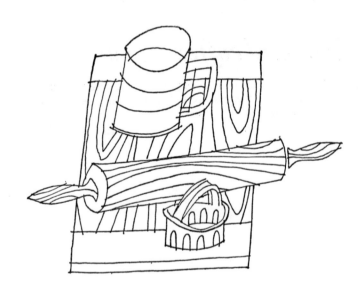

cream of cauliflower soup

1. Place stock, peppercorns, margarine, parsley, bayleaf, onion and seasoning in a saucepan. Bring to the boil and cook gently for 20 minutes.
2. Add prepared cauliflower (cut into small pieces), cook gently for 30 minutes.
3. Blend arrowroot with a little of the measured milk. Add remainder of milk to soup, stir in blended arrowroot.
4. Bring to the boil, stirring continually, cook for 3 minutes. Sieve, season and re-heat.

INGREDIENTS
1 cauliflower (medium size)
Small onion (finely chopped)
3 white peppercorns
$\frac{1}{2}$ oz. margarine
Pinch dried parsley
$\frac{1}{2}$ bay leaf
Seasoning
1 pint stock
1 pint milk
1 oz. arrowroot

cream of onion soup

1. Prepare onion and cut into thin slices. Place in a saucepan and add stock, cinnamon, seasoning and margarine.
   Bring to the boil and cook gently for 30 minutes or until onion is tender.
2. Blend flour with a little of the measured milk. Add remainder of milk to soup, stir in blended flour.
3. Bring mixture to the boil stirring continually. Cook for 3 minutes. Sieve, season and reheat.
4. Stir in cheese—serve at once.

INGREDIENTS
1 lb. onions
1 pint stock
Pinch cinnamon
Seasoning
$\frac{1}{2}$ oz. margarine
$\frac{1}{4}$ oz. Parmesan cheese
1 oz. flour
1 pint milk

tomato soup

1. Place tomatoes, onion, celery, mixed herbs, stock and seasoning in a large saucepan. Bring to the boil, cover and simmer until vegetables are cooked. Cool.
2. Blend flour with a little milk or water, add to soup. Stir until mixture boils, cook for 2–3 minutes. Sieve, season and reheat.

INGREDIENTS
1 lb. tomatoes
1 large onion (finely chopped)
1 stick celery (finely chopped)
Pinch mixed herbs
1 pint stock
Seasoning
2 teaspoonfuls flour

minestrone soup

1. Prepare onion, carrot and potato and cut into small dice. Skin and cut up tomatoes.
2. Fry prepared vegetables in margarine for a few minutes, add garlic, parsley, beans, seasoning, stock and water and bring to the boil.
3. When boiling, add spaghetti broken into short lengths. Cover with lid and cook gently for 45–60 minutes or until vegetables are tender and spaghetti is cooked. Season to taste.

Serve, sprinkled with grated Parmesan cheese.

INGREDIENTS
1 oz. haricot beans (cooked)
8 oz. tomatoes
1 small carrot
1 small potato
1 small onion
1 oz. margarine
1 pint stock
1 pint water
1 oz. spaghetti
Seasoning
1 clove garlic (finely chopped)
1 teaspoonful parsley (finely chopped)
Parmesan cheese

vegetable soup

1. Prepare vegetables (if using old carrots and large onions—chop well or grate—this reduces cooking time).
2. Place in a saucepan and add stock, seasoning, margarine, herbs, mace and meat extract. Bring to the boil and cook gently for 30 minutes or until vegetables are tender. Cool.
3. Blend flour with a little water, add to soup, stir.
4. Bring to the boil, stirring continually. Cook for 3 minutes. Sieve, add colouring, season and re-heat.

INGREDIENTS

1 lb. mixed vegetables
2 pints stock
Seasoning
½ oz. margarine
Pinch mixed herbs
1 blade mace
1 teaspoonful meat extract
1 oz. flour
Gravy browning

vegetables

preparation

Leave prepared vegetables in salt water for a short time before cooking to remove grit, insects etc. Do not soak.

Beetroot Wash. Remove leaves but do not remove roots or damage skin before cooking as this will result in loss of colour.

Broccoli, Spring Greens and Kale Remove coarse stalks.

Brussels Sprouts Trim outer leaves. Make a slit across base of stalk.

Cabbage Remove stalk and outer leaves. Cut into quarters or shred.

Carrots and Potatoes Wash and scrub with brush if necessary. Scrape or peel. Leave whole or cut into even sized pieces. e.g. halved, quartered, diced or sliced.

Cauliflower	Trim most of outer leaves. Sprig or cut into quarters. Scoop out centre stalk. Wash.
Marrow	Cut down centre. Remove seeds. Peel. Cut as required. Sprinkle with salt (this will draw some moisture from the marrow, it will then be firmer when cooked).
Onions and Shallots	Remove top, roots and skin. Leave whole or slice as required.
Peas and Broad Beans	Remove from shell.
Runner or French Beans	Remove ends and slice just before required (if limp, place ends in water for a short time before slicing).
Spinach	Prepare as for Spring Greens but wash in several changes of water to remove all grit.
Turnips and Parsnips	Wash. Peel (quite a thick portion needs to be removed). Cut old vegetables into halves or quarters.

methods of cooking

The most usual methods of cooking vegetables are boiling and steaming.

boiling

1. Use a large pan and cover with a lid if practical. Bring sufficient water to the boil and add vegetables, salt and flavouring. e.g. mint. (Spinach requires no water because enough water clings to the leaves after washing.)
2. Boil steadily until tender. Fast boiling or over-cooking will tend to make vegetables break, resulting in loss of flavour, loss of colour and vegetables becoming watery.

steaming

Carrots, potatoes, turnips, parsnips, etc. may be steamed (page 14). Cook until tender. This is a slightly slower method than boiling.

to serve vegetables

Drain well and serve very hot. A knob of butter will improve some vegetables.

Potatoes etc. may be mashed or sieved with butter or milk.

Carrots, peas, broad beans may be sieved. This makes them more digestible for children and invalids.

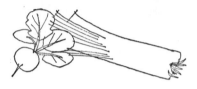

roast potatoes

1. Prepare potatoes, and cut into even size pieces. Wipe dry.
2. Place in melted fat. Bake, turning once or twice during the cooking time to brown evenly.

INGREDIENTS
2 lb. potatoes
Dripping or lard

baked potatoes

1. Scrub potatoes and make a small cut in the top. Brush skin with melted margarine. Place on baking tray. Bake.
2. When potatoes are cooked, cut through the centre, scoop out and mash well with butter and seasoning. Pile back into skin. Serve at once.

INGREDIENTS
4 medium potatoes
Margarine
Butter
Seasoning

baked stuffed potatoes

Cook as for previous recipe, adding cheese when mashing potato. Brown under grill before serving.

INGREDIENTS
4 tablespoonfuls grated cheese

creamed potatoes (oven method)

1. Peel potatoes and cut into slices $\frac{1}{4}''$ thick.
2. Place in dish with water and seasoning. Cover with foil. Bake.
3. When cooked, drain and mash with butter and milk.

INGREDIENTS
$1\frac{1}{2}$-2 lb. potatoes
$\frac{1}{2}$-$\frac{3}{4}$ pint water
Seasoning
Butter
Milk

duchess potatoes

1. Prepare potatoes and boil in salt water until cooked.
2. Drain, replace in saucepan and cover with a piece of muslin to absorb excess moisture.
3. Sieve potatoes, mix in margarine and egg. Stir thoroughly.
4. Place in spoonfuls and 'fork up' or pipe onto greased baking tray. Bake until golden brown.

INGREDIENTS
1 lb. potatoes
$\frac{1}{2}$ egg
$\frac{1}{2}$ oz. margarine
Seasoning

sauté potatoes

1. Prepare potatoes. Boil in salted water until cooked.
2. Drain, cut in $\frac{1}{4}''$ thick slices.
3. Place in a mixture of equal quantity oil and butter in frying pan. Shallow fry potato slices until golden brown, turning occasionally. Remove and drain.
Serve sprinkled with seasoning and parsley.

INGREDIENTS
1 lb. potatoes
Oil
Butter
Seasoning
Parsley (finely chopped)

83

savoury potatoes

1. Prepare potatoes and cut into ¼″ thick slices, arrange in dish.
2. Grate onion, add to stock, pour over potatoes. Dot with margarine. Season.
3. Cover with a piece of foil. Bake.

INGREDIENTS
1½-2 lb. potatoes
1 onion
¼-½ pint stock
½ oz. margarine
Seasoning

stuffed marrow

1. Prepare marrow, cut in half and cut through centre. Place in boiling water and cook until tender. (Do not overcook.) Drain.
2. Fry mushrooms and onion in butter until cooked.
3. Mix with minced meat, chopped ham, parsley, breadcrumbs, seasoning and beaten egg.
4. Place lower half of marrow in dish, pile on stuffing, cover with remaining half. Pour over a little melted butter and sprinkle with raspings. Bake.

INGREDIENTS
1 medium size marrow

Stuffing
2 oz. mushrooms (finely chopped)
1 onion (finely chopped)
1 oz. butter
½ teaspoonful chopped parsley
1½ oz. breadcrumbs
2 oz. ham
8 oz. minced cooked beef
1 egg
Seasoning

Coating
Melted butter, raspings

stuffed onions

1. Remove skin from onions, do not cut away roots. Place in boiling water and parboil for 15 minutes.
2. Remove from water, cool slightly, cut a slice from each end and ease out centre.
3. Fill cavity with sausage meat. Place stuffed onions in dish, add about ¼-½ pint water. Cover with foil. Bake.

INGREDIENTS
To each large onion allow . .
1½-2 oz. sausage meat

stuffed peppers

1. Cook peppers in boiling salted water for 5 minutes. Cut a slice from top, remove seeds and fibrous centre.
2. Place rice, bay leaf and seasoning in boiling stock. Cover pan, reduce heat and simmer until rice is cooked and stock absorbed. Remove bay leaf, add sultanas and chopped ham.
3. Drain and fill pepper with prepared mixture, replace lid, place upright in dish. Pour in $\frac{1}{4}$-$\frac{1}{2}$ pint water.
4. Top with butter, sprinkle with raspings. Cover with buttered paper. Bake.

INGREDIENTS
2 large peppers
2 oz. Patna rice
$\frac{1}{2}$ pint stock
$\frac{1}{2}$ bay leaf
2 oz. sultanas
2 oz. ham
Seasoning
Knob butter
Raspings
Water

stuffed tomatoes

1. Wash tomatoes, cut a slice from the top and remove core and juice using a teaspoon.
2. Discard core, mix butter, breadcrumbs, cheese, onion, parsley and seasoning with juice. Pack back into tomato.
3. Replace lid and arrange in dish. Cover with foil. Bake.
   Other fillings that may be used in place of cheese . . . sardine, salmon, ham, cooked cold meat, corned beef, etc.

INGREDIENTS
4-6 firm tomatoes
$1\frac{1}{2}$ oz. butter
$1\frac{1}{2}$ oz. breadcrumbs
3 oz. grated cheese
**1 teaspoonful onion
  (finely chopped)**
Pinch chopped parsley
Seasoning

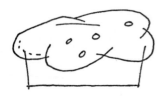

yeast mixtures

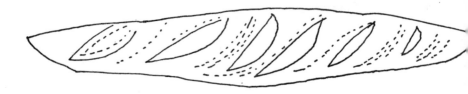

mixing the dough

When making a yeast dough, keep all the utensils and ingredients warm, this helps the yeast to produce gas, thus making the dough rise. Take special care not to overheat the mixture, this will inactivate the yeast.

Kneading   Dough is kneaded to make a soft silky mixture, it also makes an even texture mixture by distributing the gases. The mixture is brought from the outside to the centre, (using the knuckles) working into a soft smooth dough.

Proving   Leave to prove in a warm atmosphere, humid if possible.

ingredients

Flour Plain flour is always used when making up yeast mixtures, the yeast takes the place of baking powder as a raising agent.

Yeast Use fresh yeast only. Stale yeast is tinged with brown pieces, is crumbly and has a strong smell. Fresh yeast is the colour of putty. Dried yeast may be used as instructed on packet.

Fruit Wash, clean and pick over, dry. Add to mixture after the first proving.

cooking and cooling

Baking Bake in a hot oven to set the dough and a lower heat to cook it.

Testing Lift from the tin. Tap the base, if it sounds hollow and the exterior is nicely browned, cooking is complete.

Cooling Remove from tin, place on a cooling rack.

small milk loaf

1. Warm flour, sieve salt with flour.
2. Mix sugar with yeast, add warm milk and water, also beaten egg.
3. Rub fat into flour, pour in liquid and beat well with the hands until mixture is smooth. Stand in a warm place to prove. Cover with a damp cloth during this time.
4. When mixture has doubled its bulk, knead well on a floured board, halve dough. Shape each piece into a 'bolster', place in greased tins. Stand in a warm place to prove again. When mixture has risen to the top of the tin, bake.

INGREDIENTS
1 lb. plain flour
1 level teaspoonful salt
2 oz. lard
½ pint milk and water (bare measure)
1 egg
½ oz. yeast
1 teaspoonful sugar

dinner rolls

Make up mixture as for Small Milk Loaf (page 87). When mixture has been left to prove for the first time, knead well and shape into 16 even size rolls. Arrange on greased baking trays. Stand in a warm place until mixture has risen and a tight 'skin' has formed over the rolls. Brush with beaten egg. Bake.

INGREDIENTS
Small milk loaf mixture
Beaten egg

doughnuts

1. Make up as for Small Milk Loaf (page 87).
2. When mixture has been left to prove for the first time, knead well and roll out. Cut into rings (about 12) using 3″ and 2″ cutters. Leave to prove on a baking tray.
3. When proved, deep fry in hot fat turning once.
4. Toss cooked doughnuts in a mixture of sugar and cinnamon.

INGREDIENTS
8 oz. plain flour
¼ teaspoonful salt
2 oz. margarine
1 teaspoonful caster sugar
½ oz. yeast
½ egg
Milk, } **to make**
Water } **¼ pint**

Coating
Caster sugar
Cinnamon

miscellaneous

mincemeat

1. Peel, core and grate apples, chop currants, raisins, suet and almonds. Mix together.
2. Add mixed peel, lemon rind and strained juice. Stir in brown sugar, cider and mixed spice.
3. Mix very well together. Place into clean jars, cover. Store in a very cool place until required. Makes approx. 4 lb.

INGREDIENTS

8 oz. currants
12 oz. apples
8 oz. raisins
8 oz. suet
6 oz. mixed peel (finely chopped)
Juice and finely grated rind of 2 lemons
2 oz. blanched almonds
8 oz. brown sugar
1½ teaspoonfuls mixed spice
⅛ pint cider

parsley and thyme stuffing

Mix all dry ingredients together, use egg to bind. Use as required.

INGREDIENTS

1 oz. breadcrumbs
1 tablespoonful suet
2 teaspoonfuls parsley (finely chopped)
Beaten egg
Rind of ½ lemon (finely grated)
½ teaspoonful mixed herbs
¼ teaspoonful salt, pepper

sage and onion stuffing

Mix ingredients together, using egg to bind. Use as required.

INGREDIENTS

6 oz. finely grated raw onion

2 oz. breadcrumbs

$\frac{1}{2}$ teaspoonful salt

$\frac{1}{8}$ teaspoonful pepper

1 oz. margarine

2 teaspoonfuls sage (finely chopped)

Beaten egg

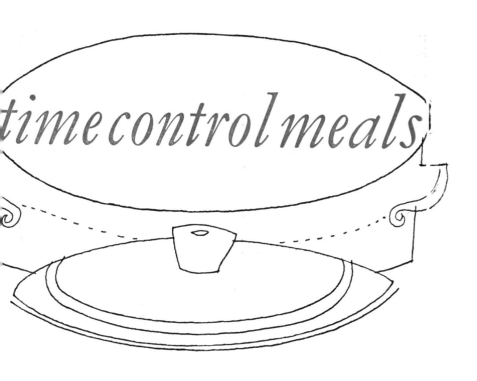

time control meals

When planning time control meals, remember the following:

1. Choose dishes which will take about the same time to cook and require the same oven temperature.

2. Add 10 minutes to the usual cooking time when calculating total cooking time required.

3. Temperature may be increased or reduced slightly and the cooking time altered accordingly.

4. If one dish of the selected menu requires less time, or a slightly lower temperature, place in the coolest part of the oven or cover with foil, this will slow down the cooking and prevent over-browning. The use of ovenware dishes also slows down the cooking compared with metal utensils.

5. Choose convenient size dishes which fit into the oven making the most use of oven space.

6. Just before or during serving the meal, cook green vegetables and, thicken sauces, etc. The use of frozen vegetables is recommended, since they are already prepared and require a minimum of cooking time.

7. Ensure that meat and fish are absolutely fresh when placed in oven, otherwise they can become completely inedible in a very short time during hot weather.

Here is a selection of time control meals, including breakfast dishes. For instructions on operation of the Time Control, oven temperatures, shelf positions and cooking times see your Instruction Card.

The menus below are intended as a guide, but with a little experience and planning your own selections may be made.

(1) **Stuffed Pork Chops** *page 50*
Savoury Potatoes *page 84*
Pineapple Upside-down
Pudding *page 63*

(3) **Roast Lamb** (3 lb joint)
Roast Potatoes *page 82*
Baked Custard *page 57*
Apple Charlotte *page 55*

(2) **Hot Pot** *page 46*
Creamed Potatoes *page 83*
Rice Pudding *page 60*
Casserole of Fruit *page 59*

(4) **Chicken Casserole** *page 44*
Creamed Potatoes *page 83*
Fruit Pie (shortcrust) *page 61*

(5) **Baked Stuffed Cod** *page 35*
Savoury Potatoes *page 84*
Baked Pudding *page 57*

time control breakfasts

(1)

1. Butter a quarter pint ovenware dish very well (one per person).
2. Remove rind from bacon and chop up. Mix with breadcrumbs and seasoning.
3. Place a layer of bacon mixture in dish. Break over egg and cover with remainder of mixture. Arrange in oven.

For each person allow:
1 egg
2 rashers bacon
2 tablespoonfuls breadcrumbs
Seasoning
Butter

(2)

Skin sausages and halve. Remove rind from bacon. Wrap each piece of sausage in a bacon rasher. Place in a 2 pint oblong ovenware dish with lard. Arrange in oven.

4 sausages
8 rashers bacon
1 oz. lard

(3)

Prick sausages, skin mushrooms. Arrange mushrooms in base of 2 pint oblong ovenware dish, place sausages on top. Add lard.
Wipe tomatoes, place in 1 pint oval ovenware dish with a little water. Cover with foil. Arrange in oven.

1 lb. sausages
4 oz. mushrooms
4 tomatoes
1 oz. lard

(4)

Place haddock in 2 pint oblong ovenware dish with milk, butter and seasoning. Cover with a piece of greased greaseproof paper. Arrange in oven.

4 pieces of
    smoked haddock
⅛ pint milk
½ oz. butter
Seasoning

candies

Nothing is more enjoyable than a box of home made candies. The following recipes are economical, and both quick and easy to prepare, no cooking being necessary. Due to the fact that the ingredients are not cooked the sweets should be eaten soon after making and not stored for long periods.

nut clusters

1. Melt chocolate in small basin over hot water.
2. Leave until cool, but still liquid. Stir in chopped nuts or coconut.
3. Allow mixture to thicken then spoon into small paper cases.

INGREDIENTS

4 oz. cooking chocolate

3 oz. chopped almonds or walnuts or

2 oz. desiccated coconut

cherry nut clusters

Make up mixture as above, but add chopped glacé cherries at stage 2.

INGREDIENTS

1 oz. glacé cherries

ginger nut clusters

Make up mixture as for Nut Clusters, but add chopped ginger at stage 2.

INGREDIENTS
1 oz. ginger

raisin nut clusters

Make up mixture as for Nut Clusters, but add chopped raisins at stage 2.

INGREDIENTS
1 oz. raisins

almond cherries

1. Knead almond paste.
2. Wrap each cherry in a portion of almond paste, form into a ball.
3. Slice top off each ball leaving cherry exposed.
4. Place in small paper cases.

INGREDIENTS
Almond paste
Glacé cherries

chocolate almond cherries

1. Make up Almond Cherries as above, but do not slice top.
2. Melt chocolate in small basin over hot water. Leave until cool, but still liquid.
3. Coat each Almond Cherry with chocolate, leave to set.
4. Place in small paper cases.

INGREDIENTS
Cooking chocolate

iced almond cherries

Make up as for Chocolate Almond Cherries, but coat with Glacé Icing (see page 38) instead of chocolate.

truffles

1. Cream butter, add essences. Stir in sieved icing sugar and ground almonds
2. Melt chocolate in small basin over hot water. Leave until cool but still liquid, beat into mixture.
3. Using icing sugar to dredge, knead up mixture. Shape into small balls. Leave in a cool place to become firm.
4. Coat with egg white, roll in vermicelli.
5. Place in small paper cases.

INGREDIENTS
8 oz. icing sugar
3 oz. butter
2 oz. ground almonds
2 oz. cooking chocolate
Almond essence
Rum essence
Icing sugar to dredge
Egg white
Chocolate vermicelli

raisin truffles

Make up mixture as above, knead in chopped raisins before shaping.

INGREDIENTS
2 oz. raisins

cherry truffles

Make up mixture as for Truffles, knead in chopped cherries before shaping.

INGREDIENTS
2 oz. glacé cherries

chocolate almond squares

1. Divide almond paste into 2 equal portions. Roll out each piece to $\frac{1}{8}$″ thickness.
2. Roll out Truffle mixture to $\frac{1}{4}$″ thickness.
3. Brush one piece of almond paste with egg white. Place Truffle mixture on top.
4. Brush Truffle mixture with egg white, top with almond paste.
5. Leave till firm. Cut into squares.
6. Place in small paper cases.

INGREDIENTS
$\frac{1}{2}$ quantity mixture as for Truffles
4 oz. almond paste
Icing sugar to dredge
Egg white

walnut creams

1. Sieve icing sugar and cream of tartar.
2. Add sufficient evaporated milk to form a stiff paste.
3. Using icing sugar to dredge, knead up mixture, adding flavouring to taste.
4. Roll out to $\frac{1}{2}''$ thickness and cut into fancy shapes.
5. Moisten top with evaporated milk, decorate with walnut halves.
6. Place in small paper cases.

INGREDIENTS
1 lb. icing sugar
$\frac{1}{4}$ teaspoonful cream of tartar
Evaporated milk
Vanilla essence
Icing sugar to dredge
Walnuts

peppermint creams

Make up mixture as above. Knead in green colouring and peppermint essence in place of vanilla essence.

INGREDIENTS
Peppermint essence
Green colouring

orange creams

Make up mixture as for Walnut Creams. Omit vanilla essence. Knead in orange colouring, and finely grated orange rind to taste.

INGREDIENTS
1 small orange
Orange colouring

lemon creams

Make up mixture as for Orange Creams using lemon colouring and finely grated lemon rind in place of orange flavouring and colouring.

INGREDIENTS
1 small lemon
Lemon colouring

orange coconut creams

1. Sieve icing sugar and cream of tartar.
2. Add orange juice, coconut and sufficient evaporated milk to form a stiff paste.
3. Using icing sugar to dredge, knead up mixture adding finely grated orange rind to taste. Knead in orange colouring.
4. Roll into small balls, decorate with a chocolate drop.
5. Place in small paper cases.

INGREDIENTS
½ lb. icing sugar
Pinch of cream of tartar
Evaporated milk
4 oz. desiccated coconut
1 small orange
Orange colouring
Chocolate drops
Icing sugar to dredge

raspberry coconut creams

Make up mixture as for Orange Coconut Creams. Use all evaporated milk instead of orange juice. Substitute raspberry essence and cochineal colouring in place of orange rind and colouring.

INGREDIENTS
Raspberry essence
Cochineal colouring
Evaporated milk

THORN

A member of the Thorn Group

TRICITY COOKERS LIMITED
NEW LANE, HAVANT, HAMPSHIRE
HAVANT 6400   STD 0701-2 6400

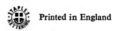 Printed in England